TRIANGLE HISTORIES

THE REVOLUTIONARY WAR

THE BATTLE OF BUNKER HILL

Scott Ingram

BLACKBIRCH®
PRESS

THOMSON

GALE

San Diego • Detroit • New York • San Francisco • Cleveland • New Haven, Conn. • Waterville, Maine • London • Munich

THOMSON

GALE

For more information, contact
The Gale Group, Inc.
27500 Drake Rd.
Farmington Hills, MI 48331-3535
Or you can visit our Internet site at http://www.gale.com

Photo credits: cover, page 5 © North Wind Picture Archives; pages 7, 15 © Library of Congress; pages 8, 10, 13, 19, 24, 25 © Bettmann/CORBIS; pages 9, 13, 17, 28 © Hulton Archive/Getty Images; page 11 © Burstein Collection/CORBIS; pages 18, 22, 26 © CORBIS; page 20 © Scala/Art Resource; page 27 © Francis G. Mayer/CORBIS

LIBRARY OF CONGRESS CATALOGING-IN-PUBLICATION DATA

Ingram, Scott (William Scott)
  The Battle of Bunker Hill / by Scott Ingram.
    p. cm. — (Triangle history of the American Revolution series.
Revolutionary War battles)
Includes bibliographical references and index.
Summary: Examines the events, aftermath, and significance of the Battle
of Bunker Hill.
  ISBN 1-56711-775-9 (hardback : alk. paper)
  1. Bunker Hill, Battle of, Boston, Mass., 1775—Juvenile literature. [1. Bunker Hill,
Battle of, Boston, Mass., 1775. 2. United States—History—Revolution, 1775-1783—
Campaigns.] I. Title. II. Series.

E241.B9 I54 2004
973.3'312—dc21   2002153091

Printed in China
10 9 8 7 6 5 4 3 2 1

CONTENTS

Preface: The American Revolution

Today, more than two centuries after the final shots were fired, the American Revolution remains an inspiring story not only to Americans, but also to people around the world. For many citizens, the well-known battles that occurred between 1775 and 1781—such as Lexington, Trenton, Yorktown, and others—represent the essence of the Revolution. In truth, however, the formation of the United States involved much more than the battles of the Revolutionary War. The creation of our nation occurred over several decades, beginning in 1763, at the end of the French and Indian War, and continuing until 1790, when the last of the original thirteen colonies ratified the Constitution.

More than two hundred years later, it may be difficult to fully appreciate the courage and determination of the people who fought for, and founded, our nation. The decision to declare independence was not made easily—and it was not unanimous. Breaking away from England—the ancestral land of most colonists—was a bold and difficult move. In addition to the emotional hardship of revolt, colonists faced the greatest military and economic power in the world at the time.

The first step on the path to the Revolution was essentially a dispute over money. By 1763 England's treasury had been drained in order to pay for the French and Indian War. British lawmakers, as well as England's new ruler, King George III, felt that the colonies should help to pay for the war's expense and for the cost of housing the British troops who remained in the colonies. Thus began a series of oppressive British tax acts and other laws that angered the colonists and eventually provoked full-scale violence.

The Stamp Act of 1765 was followed by the Townshend Acts in 1767. Gradually, colonists were forced to pay taxes on dozens of everyday goods from playing cards to paint to tea. At the same time, the colonists had no say in the passage of these acts. The more colonists complained that "taxation without representation is tyranny," the more British lawmakers claimed the right to make laws for the colonists "in all cases whatsoever." Soldiers and tax collectors were sent to the colonies to enforce the new laws. In addition, the colonists were forbidden to trade with any country but England.

Each act of Parliament pushed the colonies closer to unifying in opposition to English laws. Boycotts of British goods inspired protests and violence against tax collectors. Merchants who continued to trade with the Crown risked attacks by their colonial neighbors. The rising violence soon led to riots against British troops stationed in the colonies and the organized destruction of British goods. Tossing tea into Boston Harbor was just one destructive act. That event, the Boston Tea Party, led England to pass the so-called Intolerable Acts of 1774. The port of Boston was closed, more British troops were sent to the colonies, and many more legal rights for colonists were suspended.

Finally, there was no turning back. Early on an April morning in 1775, at Lexington Green in Massachusetts, the first shots of the American Revolution were fired. Even after the first battle, the idea of a war against England seemed unimaginable to all but a few radicals. Many colonists held out hope that a compromise could be reached. Except for the Battle of Bunker Hill and some minor battles at sea, the war ceased for much of 1775. During this time, delegates to the Continental Congress struggled to reach a consensus about the next step.

During those uncertain months, the Revolution was fought, not on a military battlefield, but on the battlefield of public opinion. Ardent rebels—especially Samuel Adams and Thomas Paine—worked tirelessly to keep the spirit of revolution alive. They stoked the fires of revolt by writing letters and pamphlets, speaking at public gatherings, organizing boycotts, and devising other forms of protest. It was their brave efforts that kept others focused on liberty and freedom until July 4, 1776. On that day, Thomas Jefferson's Declaration of Independence left no doubt about the intentions of the colonies. As John Adams wrote afterward, the "revolution began in hearts and minds not on battlefield."

As unifying as Jefferson's words were, the United States did not become a nation the moment the Declaration of Independence claimed the right of all people to "life, liberty, and the pursuit of happiness." Before, during, and after the war, Americans who spoke of their "country" still generally meant whatever colony was their home. Some colonies even had their own navies during the war, and a few sent their own representatives to Europe to seek aid for their colony alone while delegates from the Continental Congress were doing the same job for the whole United

The Minuteman statue stands in Concord, Massachusetts.

States. Real national unity did not begin to take hold until the inauguration of George Washington in 1789, and did not fully bloom until the dawn of the nineteenth century.

The story of the American Revolution has been told for more than two centuries and may well be told for centuries to come. It is a tribute to the men and women who came together during this unique era that, to this day, people the world over find inspiration in the story of the Revolution. In the words of the Declaration of Independence, these great Americans risked "their lives, their fortunes, and their sacred honor" for freedom.

5

Introduction:
"As Thick as Sheep
in a Field"

By the afternoon of June 17, 1775, the day had grown brutally hot in the area around Boston, Massachusetts. For hours, British warships in Boston Harbor and artillery in Boston had fired at colonial defenses on the Charlestown peninsula. The barrage had fallen short of the fortifications, but much of the town of Charlestown was on fire.

Above the town, on the slopes of the Charlestown peninsula, patriot soldiers from New England colonies prepared to fight. Since midnight, these untrained farmers, teachers, and craftsmen, under the command of Colonel William Prescott, had worked to dig and fortify defensive positions on Breed's Hill. The original plan had been to fortify Bunker Hill, the highest point on the peninsula. When Prescott realized that patriot cannons would not reach Boston from there, he ordered Breed's Hill fortified instead.

At dawn on June 17, when the patriots' location was spotted, the British cannons had opened fire. The shots had fallen short, but the thunderous guns created near-panic among the young soldiers. The fear had grown by the early afternoon when more than two thousand British regulars assembled at Morton's Point, near Charlestown.

On Breed's Hill the patriots had an advantage in position over their enemies, but most were exhausted from the night's work. They were also frightened. Until that day, many had never heard cannon fire. Although many were expert hunters

6

The British suffered heavy losses in their first assault on Breed's Hill.

and thus good marksmen, few had ever fired their weapons in battle. Prescott, who had fought in the French and Indian War, was concerned about how his men would respond to an attack by British troops.

By three o'clock, the British had formed traditional battle lines at the base of Breed's Hill that extended nearly a half mile across. Their sharp steel bayonets flashed wickedly in the sun. For the redcoats, however, who wore wool uniform jackets buttoned tight and carried 60-pound packs on their backs, the march uphill in the full heat of the day became a slow walk.

The patriots gripped their muskets with sweaty hands as Prescott ordered his men to hold their fire until the last possible moment. Powder and musket balls were in short supply, he said. Aim low for their legs, Prescott reminded his men, and shoot first at the men in the fanciest uniforms—those are the officers.

Finally, the patriots heard the squeak of leather and the jingle of silver buckles—the redcoats were within 100 feet. The sharp report of muskets erupted, and huge gaps appeared in the British lines. The British commander, General William Howe, lost his top four officers in the first volley. Soon the call to retreat was sounded, and the British fell back to regroup. Howe later wrote his dead and wounded men lay "as thick as sheep in a field."

In those first moments, the battle named for Bunker Hill strongly favored the patriots. The British, however, were deter-mined to continue the attack no matter what the cost. As they formed lines to charge a second time, the patriots realized that this was no hit-and-run skirmish like the one that had occurred in Concord two months earlier. It was the first true battle of the American Revolution.

7

The Call to Arms

★ ★ ★ ★ ★

England's king George III refused to let strict rule led to protests in the American colonies govern themselves.

By the spring of 1775, England and its American colonies were on the brink of war after years of disagreement. Some colonists believed that a fight for independence from England was the only course of action. Even those colonists who did not support a war demanded at least a voice in the way they were governed.

Yet King George III and the legislative branch of the British government—Parliament—refused to grant any representation to the colonies. In response, the colonies sent representatives to Philadelphia, Pennsylvania, to form their own Continental Congress.

Nowhere was the anti-British feeling stronger than in Massachusetts—especially in the port city of Boston. Ill will had grown since 1773, when colonists dumped chests of British tea into Boston Harbor to protest the tax policies of the British government. In response to the so-called Boston Tea Party, the British had ordered the port of Boston closed, and placed the entire Massachusetts colony under a military governor, General Thomas Gage. Thousands of British troops had been stationed in the city. The Boston area was under stricter British controls

8

Skirmishes between minutemen and redcoats in Massachusetts began the American Revolution.

than any other region of the American colonies. The sympathy that other colonists felt for those in Massachusetts helped to create a strong anti-British feeling from New Hampshire to South Carolina.

By 1775 most colonies had organized civilian army groups called militia. The Massachusetts militiamen, known as minutemen, were so named because they claimed they could answer the call to arms at a moment's notice. They stored weapons and supplies in central areas outside of Boston and other cities, ready to be used if the redcoats came into their region. In the spring of 1775, Gage learned of the colonists' preparations for war and requested reinforcements from England.

On April 19 the tension that had built between Great Britain and the American colonies exploded in skirmishes at Lexington and Concord, west of Boston. The violence began when Gage ordered British troops to arrest John Hancock and Samuel Adams in Lexington. Those men were on their way to Philadelphia to participate in the Continental Congress. The British troops were instructed to capture Hancock and Adams, then march to Concord to capture gunpowder, cannons, and other weapons stored at a farm outside of town.

On that April morning, Hancock and Adams were warned of the approaching British and escaped before redcoats marched onto Lexington Green at dawn. About one hundred minutemen, meanwhile, had assembled on the green. The force that the colonists faced outnumbered them ten to one. As the opposing sides stood their ground, a shot rang out. A volley of musket fire followed. Eight colonists fell dead, and ten were wounded. The militia fled in a disorganized retreat.

With the minutemen driven from Lexington, the British marched 18 miles toward Concord to take the colonists' weapons and gunpowder. They were unaware that hundreds of additional minutemen from the region were headed there to meet them. At Concord, the minutemen turned back several British charges, and then fired at the retreating redcoats from behind trees and walls.

By the afternoon of April 19, the British were in retreat to Boston as patriots harassed them from hidden positions. At the end of that crucial day, more than 270 British soldiers had been

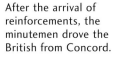

After the arrival of reinforcements, the minutemen drove the British from Concord.

Boston: Harbor of the Revolution

Colonists revolted when the British closed Boston Harbor (pictured). The closure of Boston Harbor led to American revolt.

In 1620 the first Europeans arrived in Massachusetts in the area known today as Cape Cod. By 1630 a group of settlers had migrated northwest to a well-protected harbor area with more than thirty islands. In the middle of the islands lay a 400-acre peninsula of land called Shawmut ("Living Waters") that was connected to the mainland by a thin strip of land.

By the early 1700s Shawmut, now known as Boston, had become one of the most important ports in the English colonies. The deep-water harbor, formed by waters from Massachusetts Bay as well as freshwater from the Mystic and Charles Rivers, was crowded with merchant ships and fishing vessels. Much of the initial resistance to British rule arose in Boston because its merchants were forced by the British Navigation Acts to sell or import only British-made goods carried on British ships.

By the 1740s more than twenty thousand people lived on the peninsula and the surrounding mainland. The city's pride was Long Wharf, which extended more than a half mile into the harbor and allowed the largest ships to unload cargo even during low tide. Anti-British feeling, however, grew to a fever pitch when the British closed Boston Harbor after the Boston Tea Party in 1773. That action put the colonists in the region under extreme economic hardship. In fact, it was the close of the harbor and the military rule of Boston that led directly to the first battles of the American Revolution.

killed or wounded. Word went out from Massachusetts to the surrounding colonies: The Revolution had begun.

Within 48 hours of the events at Lexington and Concord, militia units from the New England colonies began to gather in the town of Cambridge, west of Boston. Throughout May, more than seven thousand colonial soldiers assembled around Cambridge. From the south, militia from Connecticut arrived under the command of General Israel Putnam, a hero of the French and Indian War. More militia units from New Hampshire arrived under the command of Colonel John Stark.

Eventually, the various independent militia units were persuaded to support the Massachusetts Committee of Public Safety. This group was led by Dr. Joseph Warren, who had been a leader of the anti-British movement for ten years. Warren convinced the troops to form one force—a New England army. By early June the patriot militias had agreed to serve under the command of General Artemas Ward, the senior officer of the Massachusetts militia.

★

On May 10, 1775, the Second Continental Congress convened in Philadelphia.

★

British Strategy

While colonial troops assembled in Cambridge, British military leaders in Boston planned their next move. By May 25 the reinforcements requested by Gage had arrived in the city. Three generals had accompanied the troops from England. Two of the generals, William Howe and Henry Clinton, had lived and fought in the colonies. Howe was a hero of the French and Indian War who had led colonists to victory in a key battle. Clinton had been born in New York and served as an officer in the New York militia in the war. Like Gage—who had fought beside George Washington in the French and Indian War—both men agreed with the colonists' complaints and did not want to fight against them. They were officers in the British army, however, and had sworn on their personal honor to obey their king.

12

The third general, John Burgoyne, had never been to the colonies. Known as "Gentleman Johnny," he considered himself the best military strategist in the British army. He made no secret of his opinion that Gage was a poor leader.

The British reinforcements landed at Boston to find the city almost deserted. Homes were boarded up and shops were closed. Guardhouses stood on street corners at key intersections. The only civilian residents in the city were the colonists known as Loyalists—people who supported the crown. Among those who called themselves Loyalists, however, were a number who were actually patriot spies.

In June the British military leaders began to develop a plan to extend British control beyond Boston. The generals were confident that their crack units could easily defeat what Burgoyne called "the peasants." The main problem that the British faced

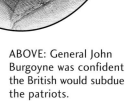

ABOVE: General John Burgoyne was confident the British would subdue the patriots.

BELOW: British troops landed in Boston in preparation for their assault on Breed's Hill.

was that the Boston peninsula was linked to the mainland by a single narrow road. On all sides, from Dorchester and Roxbury in the south to Charlestown in the north, the city was surrounded by high ground.

Gage and his generals agreed that their plan had to begin with control of the high ground. They struggled to agree, however, on which direction the initial assault should take. Some senior officers wanted to move across the Boston Neck and take Dorchester and Roxbury. From there, they said, troops could push north to Cambridge and force the patriots onto the Charlestown peninsula. Others wanted to take a shorter direct route through the Charlestown peninsula. Eventually, the leaders agreed that their troops would cross the Charles River to Charlestown. From there, Gage believed, his troops could march directly to Cambridge. Nearly as soon as the strategy was decided, however, spies brought news of the British plan to the patriots in Cambridge.

Patriots Fortify Breed's Hill

On the evening of June 16 more than twelve hundred patriot soldiers marched past the stern figure of Colonel William Prescott on the town green at Cambridge. With his gold-trimmed blue coat and white trousers tucked into polished leather boots, Prescott was the only man among the troops in a military uniform. The patriots wore homemade linen shirts and leather vests. Their ammunition pouches were slung across their chests as they marched past with muskets on their shoulders.

Prescott carried orders from commanding General Ward to march to the Charlestown peninsula. There the troops were to build fortifications on Bunker Hill, the high point on the peninsula. As night fell, the patriot force set out from Cambridge for the five-mile march to the Charlestown peninsula. Two sergeants led the troops with red lanterns to guide the men. Ox-drawn

Patriots dug in their cannons at Breed's Hill because it was closer to Boston than Bunker Hill.

wagons loaded with shovels, pickaxes, and other tools followed the soldiers.

Near midnight, the first troops crossed the narrow strip of land that led onto the Charlestown peninsula. To the left, moonlight reflected off the Mystic River. On the right, the buildings of Charlestown stood at the edge of the Charles River, which flowed sluggishly into Boston Harbor. patriots saw the masts of British warships silhouetted in the night as they lay quietly at anchor in the harbor. Directly across the water lay Boston.

As Prescott and Putnam surveyed the harbor from Bunker Hill, both men realized that although the hill was the highest point, it was not the best position. The patriots had fewer than ten small cannons. These guns were not powerful enough to reach Boston from Bunker Hill. The commander decided to move closer to the enemy and dig in at Breed's Hill. The new position was just 65 feet above the water, and it was farther from the single escape route off the peninsula. What little artillery they had, however, would reach the enemy.

Shortly after midnight, the patriot troops began to dig a redoubt—a deep rectangular trench about 160 feet long and 80 feet wide—on Breed's Hill. The dirt from the hole was piled

15

into walls. On either side of the redoubt, along the slope, soldiers constructed a breastwork from excavated dirt and any solid objects that strengthened the construction—tree branches, stones, and broken barrels.

The work had to be done quickly. Patriot leaders knew that once the British were alert to the patriot position, they would attack. Putnam sent scouts along Charlestown and Morton's Point, directly across from Boston, to make certain that the British were not aware of the patriot presence. Other patrols walked silently along the beach at the Mystic River, alert for any alarm bells on the warships.

As the night wore on, Prescott became concerned that his men would not finish the fortifications before dawn. He was even more concerned about what would happen when the British saw the patriots on Breed's Hill and attacked. His own Massachusetts men had trained in battlefield tactics, Prescott knew, but few had ever fought. Of the men from other colonies, he knew only that they were reluctant to follow orders from anyone but their local commanders. In combat, such reluctance could lead to disaster.

"Warm Fire from the Enemy"

As the first rays of daylight crept across the sky, a great deal of work remained on the redoubt and the breastwork. Prescott saw that many of his men were near exhaustion. They had received no food rations since supper the night before and had had nothing to drink except a small portion of rum on the march from Cambridge.

Prescott's concern grew as the sun rose and the patriot position was spotted by sailors on the British warship *Lively*. Soon cannons thundered across Boston Harbor. The cannonballs fell short of Breed's Hill, but the patriot soldiers were frozen in fear by what Prescott later called "warm fire from the enemy."

CHARLES TOWN

BOSTON

The bombardment continued for several hours with pauses as ships maneuvered into position to bring their shots closer. Between barrages, the patriots scrambled out of the redoubt to complete their construction. Other warships joined the *Lively* and their rounds began to land closer to the patriots' lines. Several rounds destroyed supply barrels. One round killed a patriot soldier in front of the redoubt. That death caused several soldiers to throw down their tools and flee.

Throughout the morning, Prescott urged his men to work faster. He helped build the breastworks and ordered other officers to pitch in. As the sun rose higher, Prescott saw several young soldiers collapse. Finally, Prescott sent his second-in-command, Major John Brooks, to Cambridge for reinforcements. By noon Stark's New Hampshire militia was on the way to the peninsula.

Meanwhile, across the water from Charlestown, British troops had assembled at barges on Boston's Long Wharf. Once loaded, the barges sailed around Boston Point to Morton's Point on Charlestown Peninsula, a half-mile across from Boston.

Although the British bombardment did not reach Breed's Hill, it burned Charlestown to the ground.

17

British soldiers met fierce resistance when they began their attack on Breed's Hill.

It had taken all morning for the British military leaders to reach the decision to send troops. Gage had first received word of patriot activity before dawn when Clinton had reported to him that his sentries suspected enemy activity. Clinton suggested that troops be sent at first light. Gage responded that the noise was probably just the movement of patriot sentries.

At dawn Gage went to the roof of his headquarters and saw the patriot fortifications through his telescope. The colonists had forced his hand. He could not allow them to remain dug in close enough to fire cannons into Boston. Gage did not know that the patriots had fewer than ten small field cannons and no experienced artillery units.

Gage immediately called together his senior military staff. Besides Burgoyne, Clinton, and Howe, the staff was joined by General Hugh Percy, the officer who had fought against the minutemen on the bloody retreat from Concord. Unlike Burgoyne, Percy did not consider the patriots "peasants." He knew that they would fight fiercely.

The Battle of Bunker Hill

Along with Clinton, Percy favored a plan in which the British forces would sail up the Mystic River, circle around behind the patriots, and land on Charlestown Neck. This move would cut off Prescott's troops from reinforcements in Cambridge. Gage, always a cautious leader, argued against the plan because he did not know how many patriot troops were dug in on Breed's Hill.

Howe also disagreed with the plan because he felt that the British ships could not get close enough to land troops on the marshy banks of the Mystic River near the Charlestown Neck. He favored a plan that would send British troops through Charlestown itself. Percy warned that fighting colonists in the streets of a city was an invitation to another loss like that at Concord. "Whoever looks on these people as an irregular mob will find himself much mistaken," he said.

In the end, Gage ordered Howe to lead the British troops to Morton's Point. From there, the redcoats would attack the patriots head-on in the traditional European battle style. Gage ordered Clinton and Percy to remain in Boston with reinforcements. Finally, he assigned Burgoyne to command the British artillery from Copp's Hill in Boston. Burgoyne viewed the assignment as an insult. A general who considered himself superior to his fellow officers, he believed his proper role was on the battlefield itself.

By one o'clock Howe and about twenty-five hundred British regulars had landed at Morton's Point. The redcoats formed ranks and marched to the base of Breed's Hill. There, as the twelve hundred or so thirsty, exhausted patriots watched, the British enjoyed a midday meal.

As the redcoats ate, cannon fire from Burgoyne's guns and the warships kept up a steady barrage. Instead of regular iron

British general Thomas Gage respected the Americans' fighting spirit.

cannonballs, some guns were loaded with hollow, flaming shot. Several fiery blasts hit buildings in Charlestown, and soon many homes were in flames. The few residents there fled toward Cambridge.

The Bloody Afternoon

By mid-afternoon, Prescott's men had been without food and water for more than fifteen hours. Added to the physical exhaustion was the fear that had spread among the young patriots as they now realized that they were about to fight the most

The arrival of Dr. Joseph Warren (far left, with sword) gave the patriots new confidence.

powerful army in the world. It was an army, they saw, whose soldiers were so confident of victory that they relaxed at a midday meal in front of their enemies. The patriots' morale improved slightly when Warren arrived unexpectedly at the redoubt. The wealthy doctor and political leader explained that he had come to volunteer in the fight—not as an officer, but on the front lines as a regular soldier. His bravery and appeal to the troops' patriotism brought desperately needed energy.

The patriots received more good news when Stark and the New Hampshire men arrived. As the redcoats finished their meal, Stark and his units worked quickly to strengthen a pasture fence that extended from the breastwork to the Mystic River. The fresh New Hampshire soldiers added posts and rails to the old fence and stuffed it with hay to provide cover. They rebuilt a

The Rules of War

★ ★ ★ ★ ★

It might seem strange that British soldiers ate a meal directly under the guns of the patriots before the Battle of Bunker Hill began. In modern wars no soldiers would risk leaving themselves open to enemy fire that way. Warfare in the eighteenth century, however, was fought according to rules very different from rules of warfare today.

In the 1700s the main objective of a battle was to force an enemy to move from its position. Mass destruction in battle was almost always avoided. Small advantages were the objective. Total slaughter of an enemy was considered overkill—a violation of the rules.

Battles began only when the opposing sides had taken positions in a clearly visible field. Once the order to march was given, troops advanced toward opponents in rows. They paused only to fire or reload when ordered. "Fire at will," the order for individuals to reload and fire as quickly as possible, was almost never given during the Revolution.

Battle tactics such as snipers, sneak attacks, and commando-style raids were considered uncivilized. In fact, it was the Native Americans' use of such tactics that led many European to consider them "savages." Thus, even though the patriot cannons could easily have slaughtered the British while they ate, to do so would have violated the widely accepted rules of engagement during that time.

collapsed stone wall on the Mystic River beach for added protection. This, they hoped, would prevent the British troops from circling behind Breed's Hill to surround the redoubt.

At three o'clock about one thousand British troops began a double-time march from Morton's Point along the banks of the

Colonel General William Prescott ordered his troops to fire when the redcoats drew near.

Mystic River to attack the left side—or flank—of the patriot positions. There the New Hampshire men waited. Another eleven hundred soldiers under Howe started up the hill toward the redoubt in the center of the patriot line. The British wore heavy red coats made of wool and carried 60-pound packs. Regulations required the men to button their coats to the top button. The British were immediately slowed in their march as waded through tall grass and stumbled over low stone pasture walls on the unbearably hot afternoon.

Behind the redoubt and breastworks, patriots watched the British move slowly toward them. Patriot officers walked behind the men and told them to hold their fire until the order to fire was given. Gunpowder was in short supply, and no shots could be wasted. As the British moved closer and the patriots anxiously squeezed their weapons, Prescott called out, "Don't fire until you see the whites of their eyes!"

When the order was finally given, the British were within 100 feet of the patriot lines. The patriot fire was deadly. The British lines broke as one redcoat after another spun and dropped. Near the

The Battle of Bunker Hill

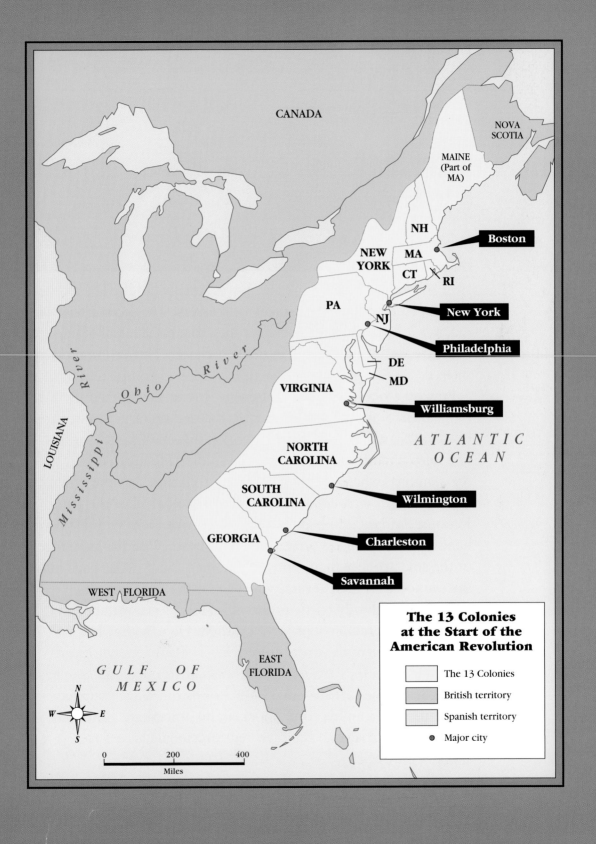

CANADA

NOVA
SCOTIA

MAINE
(Part of
MA)

NH

MA

Boston

NEW
YORK

CT

RI

PA

NJ

New York

DE

Philadelphia

MD

VIRGINIA

Williamsburg

*ATLANTIC
OCEAN*

NORTH
CAROLINA

SOUTH
CAROLINA

Wilmington

GEORGIA

Charleston

Savannah

LOUISIANA

Mississippi

Ohio River

River

WEST FLORIDA

EAST
FLORIDA

*GULF OF
MEXICO*

N
W E
S

0   200   400
Miles

The 13 Colonies
at the Start of the
American Revolution

The 13 Colonies

British territory

Spanish territory

• Major city

Boston residents watched the battle from their rooftops.

river, patriot fire on the flank attack was equally deadly. The musket fire ripped through the first row of soldiers. The second row of redcoats attempted to fire back, but they, too, faced a hail of musket balls. Dozens of officers fell in the first charge. Patriot fire mowed them down like grass, and the attack stopped completely.

Prescott stood in the thick of enemy fire as he directed the fire of his men. Stark, too, kept his men focused on targets. Putnam, however, saw that on the breastworks, the small field cannons had been abandoned by all but one soldier. He hurried over to the cannons, where the patriot soldier told him that the powder cartridge bags were too large to fit into the barrel of the gun. Furious, Putnam grabbed the bags and broke them with his bare hands as enemy bullets whizzed past his head. With the assistance of the sole artillery man, Putnam rammed the powder bags into the cannon and fired several volleys into the British ranks.

Below the bloody battle on Breed's Hill, Howe watched in horror as his crack troops were crushed. He saw that had no choice but to give the order to retreat. The patriots whooped and cheered as they realized that they had stopped an assault by the fearsome British army. Over in Boston, Gage watched the slaughter from his roof. Shocked, he immediately ordered Clinton to take several hundred reinforcements across to support Howe.

The Battle of Bunker Hill

For his part, Howe was not ready to stop the attack after one failed assault. At the base of Breed's Hill, he ordered his troops to reform within five minutes. For this attack, he allowed them to remove their coats and leave their packs behind. This charge, Howe said, would concentrate on what he believed was a weak spot between the redoubt and the breastworks. There would be no attempt to flank the enemy.

The second charge up Breed's Hill was even more difficult than the first for the British. Although the soldiers had left their packs behind, they moved more slowly as they tripped over dead bodies. This time, the patriot soldiers were more relaxed as they held their fire and waited. The British attempted to fire and reload quickly as they approached the redoubt. Because they were moving uphill, however, most shots went high over the patriot ranks. Finally, when the British line was within 50 feet, the patriots opened up with a roar of muskets.

To Howe, it seemed impossible that the second charge could be worse than the first, but it was. As their comrades fell around them, panic set in among the British. Before Howe even ordered a retreat, his troops began to run back down Breed's Hill. Howe,

Redcoats panicked as their second charge up Breed's Hill failed.

Although they had lost many men, British troops took Breed's Hill in their third assault.

an officer with many years of experience, later said, "There was a moment I never felt before."

If the battle on Breed's Hill had ended after second British charge, it would have been considered a great American victory. By that time, however, the patriots had used almost all of their powder, and Clinton had arrived with several hundred reinforcements. The patriots had been without food or water for nearly twenty-four hours, they had worked for more than twelve hours to construct defenses, and they had then turned back two charges of the British army. They had little left to give.

Incredibly, the once-confident British soldiers were in worse shape than the patriots. Most of the officers who had led the charges were dead. More than one thousand regular troops were dead or wounded. Those who had survived the two charges were near shock. Yet Howe refused to admit defeat. As the reinforcements landed, Howe walked among his men. "Fight, conquer, or die!" he shouted.

For the third time, the British assembled to charge up Breed's Hill. In addition to Clinton's reinforcements, several large artillery pieces had arrived from Boston. Howe ordered his reluctant men to pull the cannons up the hill.

26

Behind the patriot fortifications, Prescott urged his men to hold on. If the redcoats could be turned back once more, he said, they would not charge again. Slowly, the British marched past their fallen comrades. On either side of their ranks, the cannons rolled with them. This time, the British soldiers held their fire. The only fire came from the cannons, which were stopped, loaded, and fired at regular intervals. On this third attempt, the British came with 20 feet of the patriot lines before Prescott gave the order to fire. A deadly volley came from behind the patriot lines and staggered the redcoats' column. This time, however, the soldiers continued forward with bayonets aimed squarely at the patriots.

Soon the fierce British infantrymen were over the walls. They slashed and stabbed with their bayonets as the patriots swung their own muskets like clubs. Patriots whose muskets were knocked away fought with their fists until they were run through with a 2-foot bayonet. A few patriots had enough powder for

The British used their bayonets in hand-to-hand combat, as depicted in this painting of the death of Dr. Warren.

Dr. Joseph Warren: A True Patriot

Because he died at Bunker Hill, early in the Revolution, Joseph Warren is an often forgotten figure in the war. Born in 1741 in Roxbury near Boston, Warren graduated from Harvard in 1759. He then studied medicine and began a practice in 1764. Warren was the family doctor of John and Abigail Adams for several years.

When the hated Stamp Act was passed by the British Parliament in 1765, Warren published several articles in local papers that opposed the legislation. His work drew the attention of Samuel Adams, the leader of anti-British activity in Boston, and the two became close friends.

Like Adams, Warren continued to publish anti-British articles throughout the 1760s and early 1770s. To protect his family from reper-cussions, he signed many of his articles simply "A True Patriot." Eventually, however, his activities became well known, and he was called "the crazy doctor" by Loyalists in Boston.

Warren is probably best known as the man who signaled Paul Revere from the North Church to begin his ride to Lexington. On

Dr. Joseph Warren.

the day of the battle, Warren walked along Lexington Road to assist those who were wounded by the British.

At Cambridge, in the spring of 1775, Warren was named second major-general of the Massachusetts militia, despite the fact that he had never fought in a battle. On June 16 he passed commanding General Ward's order to Prescott to fortify Bunker Hill. When he heard the British troops had landed at Charlestown the next day, he rode to Breed's Hill. Prescott requested Warren stay out of the action, but he refused. Warren wanted to go where the danger was at its peak. He sought to learn to fight under well-tried officers. His arrival at the redoubt brought cheers from the tired troops. By all accounts, Warren fought fiercely and was one of the last to retreat.

Warren's death deprived the colonists of one of their most respected leaders. Though often forgotten today, many histo-rians agree that had he lived, Warren might have occupied a place in history with men such as Jefferson, Adams, and Washington.

another shot. Some fired nails when they ran out of musket balls. As Prescott slashed the redcoats surrounding him with his sword, some men threw rocks at the British, who marched steadily onward through the defenses on Breed's Hill.

Finally, there was no choice. Prescott ordered a retreat and his men scrambled toward the higher ground of Bunker Hill, then reformed ranks and marched quickly toward the Charlestown Neck. Most patriot casualties in the battle occurred in the retreat. The losses would have been greater had it not been for Stark and Putnam, who organized the New Hampshire men to stand and fight as their comrades withdrew. During the confusion of the retreat, Warren was killed by a musket ball to the back of his head.

By 5:30 the battle was over. British forces stood on Bunker Hill and watched the patriots march back to Cambridge. In most battles, they would have pursued and captured an enemy force in retreat. Losses had been so heavy that day, however, that Howe and Clinton could not afford to risk more casualties.

Epilogue

For several days after the battle of Bunker Hill the air around Boston smelled of smoke and dead bodies. Many colonists in the area had heard and seen the battle, yet no one could say for sure who won. Technically, because the British forced the patriots to retreat, they were considered the victors. Yet the losses suffered by the British were more than twice those suffered by the patriots. More than one thousand British soldiers were killed or wounded in the battle. About one-eighth of all the British officers killed during the entire Revolution died that bloody afternoon. The patriots had about four hundred casualties, most after the order to retreat was given. "I wish we could sell them another hill at the same price," said one patriot officer.

All of the patriot leaders—Prescott, Stark, and Putnam—survived the war. Among the British leaders, Gage suffered as a

★

In August 1775 King George III issued a Proclamation of Rebellion, which acknowledged that the colonies were in revolt.

★

result of the battle. Burgoyne wrote lengthy letters to Parliament that blamed him for the enormous losses. Within a month, Gage was recalled to England and left the military in disgrace. Howe replaced him as military governor. Both he and Clinton shared command of British forces in America for several years before they too were recalled.

For the colonists around Boston, there was little doubt that whatever the outcome of the battle, nothing would ever be the same in their relations with England. In Braintree, south of Boston, Abigail Adams had heard the roar of cannons. On June 18 she wrote to her husband John who was a delegate to the Continental Congress. She described what she knew of the battle and called it "the decisive day...on which the fate of America depends."

Glossary

artillery mounted guns, usually cannons, positioned on land

barrage a prolonged period of artillery fire

bayonets a long knifelike weapon attached to the end of a musket or rifle

breastworks shoulder high walls used for defense

flank the side of a fighting position

fortification something constructed for defense

militia a civilian fighting force

minutemen the nickname of Massachusetts militia

patriots soldiers who fought against the British in the American Revolution

peninsula land surrounded on three sides by water

redcoats nickname given to British soldiers

redoubt an enclosed defensive position

skirmish a brief battle

strategy a plan of action

For More Information

Books

Harris, John. *America Rebels*. Boston: Boston Globe, 1976.

Ketchum, Richard. *Decisive Day: The Battle for Bunker Hill*. New York: Owl Books, 1999.

Kirby, Phillipa. *Glorious Days, Dreadful Days: The Battle of Bunker Hill*. Austin, TX: Steck-Vaughn, 1993.

Massachusetts Historical Society. *The Battle of Bunker Hill: Picture Book*. Boston: Massachusetts Historical Society, 1968.

Website

"The Decisive Day is Come"
http://www.masshist.org/bh/
Extensive website from the Massachusetts Historical Society with original source material, maps, and biographies.

Index

The Battle of Bunker Hill